W9-ASR-788

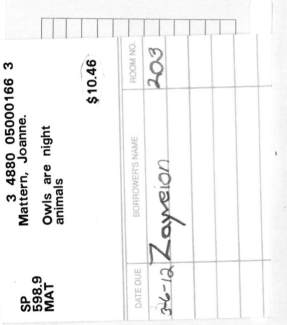

WEEKLY WR READER
EARLY LEARNING LIBRARY

Owls Are Night Animals

Los búhos son animales nocturnos

by/por Joanne Mattern

Reading consultant/Consultora de lectura: Susan Nations, M.Ed., author, literacy coach, consultant in literacy development/autora, tutora de alfabetización, consultora de desarrollo de la lectura

Science and curriculum consultant/Consultora de ciencias y contenido curricular: Debra Voege, M.A., science and math curriculum resource teacher/maestra de recursos curriculares de ciencias y matemáticas

Please visit our web site at: www.garethstevens.com
For a free color catalog describing Weekly Reader® Early Learning Library's list
of high-quality books, call 1-877-445-5824 (USA) or 1-800-387-3178 (Canada).
Weekly Reader® Early Learning Library's fax: (414) 336-0164.

SP
598.9
MAT
C-1
10.46

Library of Congress Cataloging-in-Publication Data

Mattern, Joanne, 1963-
 [Owls are night animals. Spanish & English]
 Owls are night animals = Los búhos son animales nocturnos / by/por Joanne Mattern.
  p. cm. — (Night animals = Animales nocturnos)
 Includes bibliographical references and index.
 ISBN-13: 978-0-8368-8045-8 (lib. bdg.)
 ISBN-13: 978-0-8368-8052-6 (softcover)
 1. Owls—Juvenile literature. I. Title. II. Title: Búhos son animales nocturnos.
 QL696.S83M38518   2007
 598.9'7—dc22   2006036659

This edition first published in 2007 by
Weekly Reader® Early Learning Library
A Member of the WRC Media Family of Companies
330 West Olive Street, Suite 100
Milwaukee, Wisconsin 53212 USA

Editor: Tea Benduhn
Art direction: Tammy West
Cover design and page layout: Scott M. Krall
Picture research: Diane Laska-Swanke
Spanish translation: Tatiana Acosta and Guillermo Gutiérrez

Picture credits: Cover, title page © Yuri Shibnev/naturepl.com; p. 5 © Raymond Gehman/National Geographic Image Collection; p. 7 © Tom Vezo/naturepl.com; p. 9 © Tom and Pat Leeson; p. 11 © Kevin J. Keatley/naturepl.com; p. 13 © Wendy Dennis/Visuals Unlimited; p. 15 © Kim Taylor/naturepl.com; pp. 17, 19 © Joe McDonald/ Visuals Unlimited; p. 21 © Joe & Mary Ann McDonald/Visuals Unlimited

Printed in the United States of America

1 2 3 4 5 6 7 8 9 10 10 09 08 07 06

Note to Educators and Parents

Reading is such an exciting adventure for young children! They are beginning to integrate their oral language skills with written language. To encourage children along the path to early literacy, books must be colorful, engaging, and interesting; they should invite the young reader to explore both the print and the pictures.

The *Night Animals* series is designed to help children read about creatures that are active during the night. Each book explains what a different night animal does during the day, how it finds food, and how it adapts to its nocturnal life.

Each book is specially designed to support the young reader in the reading process. The familiar topics are appealing to young children and invite them to read — and reread — again and again. The full-color photographs and enhanced text further support the student during the reading process.

In addition to serving as wonderful picture books in schools, libraries, homes, and other places where children learn to love reading, these books are specifically intended to be read within an instructional guided reading group. This small group setting allows beginning readers to work with a fluent adult model as they make meaning from the text. After children develop fluency with the text and content, the books can be read independently. Children and adults alike will find these books supportive, engaging, and fun!

— Susan Nations, M.Ed., author/literacy coach/
consultant in literacy development

Nota para los maestros y los padres

¡Leer es una aventura tan emocionante para los niños pequeños! A esta edad están comenzando a integrar su manejo del lenguaje oral con el lenguaje escrito. Para animar a los niños en el camino de la lectura incipiente, los libros deben ser coloridos, estimulantes e interesantes; deben invitar a los jóvenes lectores a explorar la letra impresa y las ilustraciones.

Animales nocturnos es una nueva colección diseñada para que los jóvenes lectores conozcan a algunos animales que están activos durante la noche. Cada libro presenta a un animal diferente, y explica lo que hace durante el día, cómo encuentra comida y cómo se adapta a su vida nocturna.

Cada libro está especialmente diseñado para ayudar a los jóvenes lectores en el proceso de lectura. Los temas familiares llaman la atención de los niños y los invitan a leer una y otra vez. Las fotografías a todo color y el tamaño de la letra ayudan aún más al estudiante en el proceso de lectura.

Además de servir como maravillosos libros ilustrados en escuelas, bibliotecas, hogares y otros lugares donde los niños aprenden a amar la lectura, estos libros han sido especialmente concebidos para ser leídos en un grupo de lectura guiada. Este contexto permite que los lectores incipientes trabajen con un adulto que domina la lectura mientras van determinando el significado del texto. Una vez que los niños dominan el texto y el contenido, el libro puede ser leído de manera independiente. ¡Estos libros les resultarán útiles, estimulantes y divertidos a niños y a adultos por igual!

— Susan Nations, M.Ed., autora/tutora de alfabetización/
consultora de desarrollo de la lectura

A spooky **hoot** fills the night air.
Who . . . Whoo . . . Whooo . . .
do you hear? It is an owl!

Un escalofriante **ulular** llena el
aire de la noche. ¡Uu...! ¡Uuu...!
¡Uuuu...! ¿Qué es lo que suena
así? ¡Es un búho!

Owls **hunt** at night. They are
carnivores. Carnivores are
animals that eat meat. Owls
eat mice and worms and many
other kinds of small animals.

Los búhos **cazan** de noche.
Son **carnívoros**. Los carnívoros
son animales que comen carne.
Los búhos comen ratones y
gusanos y muchos otros tipos
de pequeños animales.

Many parts of an owl's body help it hunt. **Feathers** cover its ears, but an owl still has excellent hearing.

Muchas partes de su cuerpo ayudan al búho a cazar. Aunque sus orejas están cubiertas de **plumas**, el oído del búho es excelente.

An owl can turn its head toward any sound. Its head can turn around very far. An owl can look behind itself. It can even turn its head upside down!

Un búho es capaz de mover la cabeza en dirección a cualquier sonido. La cabeza de un búho puede girar mucho hacia los lados. Un búho es capaz de ver lo que tiene detrás. ¡Puede incluso poner la cabeza del revés!

Owls also have very big eyes. Their eyes help them see in the dark. An owl can see a small animal moving along the ground.

Los ojos de un búho son muy grandes. Lo ayudan a ver en la oscuridad. Un búho es capaz de ver a un pequeño animal que se mueva por el suelo.

Owls have thick feathers on their wings. Thick feathers help the owl fly very quietly. An owl can easily sneak up on its **prey**.

Los búhos tienen gruesas plumas en las alas. Esas gruesas plumas les permiten volar en silencio. Un búho puede acercarse fácilmente a su **presa** sin que ésta lo oiga.

15

Owls have strong claws called **talons**. They reach down and grab prey with their talons. Owls are strong night animals.

Los búhos tienen unas fuertes uñas llamadas **garras**. Usan sus garras para alcanzar y atrapar a sus presas. Los búhos son unos animales nocturnos muy fuertes.

talons/garras

When an owl sees prey, it **swoops** down to grab it. Then the owl carries the prey off to eat it.

Cuando un búho ve a una presa, se **abate** sobre ella para atraparla. Después, se la lleva para comérsela.

Whoosh! Swoop! Whooo … Do you hear the night wind? Look around. It might be an owl.

¡Uu...! ¡Uuu...! ¡Uuuu...! ¿Oyes el viento de la noche? Mira bien. Podría ser un búho.

Glossary/Glosario

carnivores — animals that eat meat

hunt — to find and kill other animals for food

prey — an animal that is hunted by another animal

swoops — flies downward very quickly

talons — long, sharp claws on a large bird's feet

---

abatirse — lanzarse un ave en picado a gran velocidad

carnívoros — animales que comen carne

cazar — buscar y matar a otros animales para comérselos

garras — uñas largas y afiladas de un ave de gran tamaño

presa — animal que es cazado por otro animal

For More Information/Más información

Books

Owls. Animal Kingdom (series). Julie Murray (ABDO Publishing)

Owls. Animals That Live in the Forest (series). JoAnn Early Macken (Gareth Stevens)

Owls. Woodland Animals (series). Emily Rose Townsend (Pebble Books)

Owls: *Flat-Faced Flyers.* Wild World of Animals (series). Adele D. Richardson (Bridgestone Books)

Libros

El búho. Salvajes (series). Deborah Kops (Blackbirch Press)

La lechuza. ¿Qué está despierto? (series). Patricia Whitehouse (Heinemann/Raintree)

Las lechucitas. Martin Waddell (Santillana USA)

Lechuzas. Zoobooks (series). Timothy L. Biel and John Bonnett Wexo (Wildlife Education, Ltd.)

Soy veloz y silenciosa, fiera y cubierta de plumas. Cazo por la noche: ¿Quién soy? Moira Butterfield (Combel)

Index/Índice

About the Author

Joanne Mattern has written more than 150 books for children. She has written about unusual animals, sports, history, world cities, and many other topics. Joanne also works in her local library. She lives in New York State with her husband, three daughters, and assorted pets. She enjoys animals, music, reading, going to baseball games, and visiting schools to talk about her books.

Información sobre la autora

Joanne Mattern ha escrito más de ciento cincuenta libros para niños. Ha escrito textos sobre animales extraños, deportes, ciudades del mundo, dinosaurios y muchos otros temas. Además, Joanne trabaja en la biblioteca de su comunidad. Vive en el estado de Nueva York con su esposo, sus tres hijas y varias mascotas. A Joanne le gustan los animales, la música, ir al béisbol, leer y hacer visitas a las escuelas para hablar de sus libros.